Multiplication & Division Quick Starts

Editor: Mary Dieterich
Proofreaders: Margaret Brown and April Albert

COPYRIGHT © 2019 Mark Twain Media, Inc.

ISBN 978-1-62223-773-9

Printing No. CD-405039

Mark Twain Media, Inc., Publishers
Distributed by Carson-Dellosa Publishing LLC

Visit www.carsondellosa.com

Table of Contents

Introduction to the Teacher 1

Multiplication 2
    Multiplication Models.................... 2
    Multiples 3
    Multiplying by a Single Digit 5
    Multiplying by 10 6
    Multiplying by Two Digits............... 8
    Multiplying by Three Digits 9
    Multiplying Integers 11
    Multiplying by 100, 1,000,
        or More 12
    Multiplying With Decimals 13
    Multiplying a Fraction by a
        Fraction................................. 14
    Multiplying Fractions &
        Whole Numbers..................... 16
    Multiplying Mixed Numbers......... 17
    Multiplying Fractions & Mixed
        Numbers: A Shortcut.............. 19
    Multiplication Review.................. 20

Division.. 22
    Dividing Made Easier: Factors 22
    Division Models 23
    Dividing by Single Digits............. 24
    Remainders................................ 26
    Dividing by Two Digits 27
    Dividing by 10............................. 29
    Dividing by 100 or 1,000 30

    Dividing by Three Digits 31
    Dividing Integers 32
    Converting Fractions to
        Decimals............................... 34
    Dividing With Decimals 36
    Dividing With Fractions:
        Reciprocals 38
    Dividing by Fractions.................. 39
    Dividing Whole Numbers &
        Mixed Numbers..................... 40
    Division Review.......................... 42

Multiplication & Division
  Word Problems........................... 44
    Multiplication Word Problems...... 44
    Division Word Problems.............. 48
    Mixed-Operation Word
        Problems............................... 52

Answer Keys 55

Bibliography................................... 62

Introduction to the Teacher

Quick Starts help students prepare for the day's lesson while reviewing what they have previously learned. The short warm-up activities presented in this book provide teachers and parents with activities to help students practice the skills they have already learned. Each page contains two to four Quick Starts. Used at the beginning of class, Quick Starts help students focus on multiplication and division skills.

Multiplication & Division Quick Starts includes multiplication and division with whole numbers, fractions, and decimals, as well as word problems. They can be used in any order to best meet your teaching needs. Assume that all fractions should be reduced to lowest terms unless otherwise instructed.

Suggestions for use:

- Copy and cut apart enough Quick Starts to give students one activity each day at the beginning of class.

- Give each student a copy of the entire page or pages to complete day by day. Students can keep the completed pages in a three-ring binder to use as a resource for review.

- Make transparencies of individual Quick Starts and complete the activities as a group.

- Provide extra copies of Quick Starts in your learning center for students to complete at random when they have spare time.

- Keep some Quick Starts on hand to use as fill-ins when the class has a few extra minutes before lunch or dismissal.

Multiplication

Multiplication Models 1

Use multiplication of rows and columns to determine how many figures each model is composed of.

1. Rows _____
   Columns _____
   Total Figures _____

2. Rows _____
   Columns _____
   Total Figures _____

Multiplication Models 2

Use multiplication of rows and columns to determine how many figures the model is composed of.

Rows _____
Columns _____
Total Figures _____

Multiplication Models 3

Use multiplication of rows and columns to determine how many figures each model is composed of.

1. Rows _____
   Columns _____
   Total Figures _____

2. Rows _____
   Columns _____
   Total Figures _____

Multiplication Models 4

Use multiplication of rows and columns to determine how many figures the model is composed of.

Rows _____
Columns _____
Total Figures _____

Multiplication

Multiplication Models 5

Draw your own model to show the number 48.

Rows _____
Columns _____
Total Figures _____

Multiples 1

A **multiple** is the product when one number is multiplied by another number. Find the first ten multiples of 6.

1. 6 x 1 = _____ **2.** 6 x 2 = _____

3. 6 x 3 = _____ **4.** 6 x 4 = _____

5. 6 x 5 = _____ **6.** 6 x 6 = _____

7. 6 x 7 = _____ **8.** 6 x 8 = _____

9. 6 x 9 = _____ **10.** 6 x 10 = _____

Multiples 2

Find the first ten multiples of 8.

1. 8 x 1 = _____ **2.** 8 x 2 = _____

3. 8 x 3 = _____ **4.** 8 x 4 = _____

5. 8 x 5 = _____ **6.** 8 x 6 = _____

7. 8 x 7 = _____ **8.** 8 x 8 = _____

9. 8 x 9 = _____ **10.** 8 x 10 = _____

Multiples 3

Find the first ten multiples of 11.

1. 11 x 1 = _____ **2.** 11 x 2 = _____

3. 11 x 3 = _____ **4.** 11 x 4 = _____

5. 11 x 5 = _____ **6.** 11 x 6 = _____

7. 11 x 7 = _____ **8.** 11 x 8 = _____

9. 11 x 9 = _____ **10.** 11 x 10 = _____

Multiplication

Multiples 4

List the next five multiples of the following numbers.

1. 2 _____

2. 3 _____

3. 4 _____

4. 5 _____

5. 7 _____

6. 9 _____

Multiples 5

List the next five multiples of the following numbers.

1. 10 _____

2. 14 _____

3. 20 _____

4. 18 _____

5. 12 _____

6. 25 _____

Multiples 6

Write Yes or No to answer the questions below.

1. Is 24 a multiple of 6? _____

2. Is 18 a multiple of 4? _____

3. Is 32 a multiple of 8? _____

4. Is 42 a multiple of 5? _____

5. Is 15 a multiple of 7? _____

6. Is 60 a multiple of 12? _____

Multiples 7

It is important to know that if any number is multiplied by 0, the product will be 0. If any number is multiplied by 1, the product will be that number.

1. $8 \times 0 =$ ____   **2.** $8 \times 1 =$ ____

3. $7 \times 0 =$ ____   **4.** $7 \times 1 =$ ____

5. $12 \times 0 =$ ____   **6.** $12 \times 1 =$ ____

7. $2 \times 0 =$ ____   **8.** $2 \times 1 =$ ____

9. $5 \times 0 =$ ____   **10.** $5 \times 1 =$ ____

Multiplication

Multiplying by a Single Digit 1

Solve the multiplication problems.

1. 223
    x 3

2. 114
    x 2

3. 323
    x 3

4. 419
    x 4

Multiplying by a Single Digit 2

Solve the multiplication problems.

1. 676
    x 5

2. 912
    x 2

3. 927
    x 4

4. 299
    x 6

Multiplying by a Single Digit 3

Solve the multiplication problems.

1. 771
    x 9

2. 515
    x 7

3. 249
    x 3

4. 634
    x 4

Multiplying by a Single Digit 4

Solve the multiplication problems.

1. 999
    x 9

2. 101
    x 7

3. 844
    x 5

4. 398
    x 8

Multiplication

Multiplying by a Single Digit 5

Rewrite the problems in a vertical format and solve.

1. 708 x 6 =

2. 902 x 4 =

3. 307 x 8 =

4. 402 x 6 =

Multiplying by 10 1

Multiplying a number by 10 essentially moves the number over to the left one place value. For example, 245 x 10 becomes 2,450. Solve the following problems quickly by inspection without going through all the steps of multiplication.

1. 75	**2.** 145	**3.** 900	**4.** 2,240
x 10	x 10	x 10	x 10

Multiplying by 10 2

Solve the following problems quickly by inspection without going through all the steps of multiplication.

1. 313	**2.** 555	**3.** 1,000	**4.** 102
x 10	x 10	x 10	x 10

Multiplication

Multiplying by 10 3

Solve the following problems quickly by inspection without going through all the steps of multiplication.

1.	25	**2.**	150	**3.**	800	**4.**	2,250
	x 10		x 10		x 10		x 10

Multiplying by 10 4

Solve the following problems quickly by inspection without going through all the steps of multiplication.

1.	13,000	**2.**	825	**3.**	50	**4.**	175
	x 10		x 10		x 10		x 10

Multiplying by 10 5

Solve the following problems quickly by inspection without going through all the steps of multiplication.

1. 32 x 10 = _____

2. 78 x 10 = _____

3. 689 x 10 = _____

4. 325 x 10 = _____

Multiplication

Multiplying by Two Digits 1

Solve. Remember to write any carry-overs atop the column to which they apply.

1.   231
     x 23

2.   404
     x 11

3.   122
     x 42

4.   818
     x 10

Multiplying by Two Digits 2

Solve the multiplication problems.

1.   665
     x 78

2.   799
     x 34

3.   1,200
     x   14

4.   7,625
     x   51

Multiplying by Two Digits 3

Solve the multiplication problems.

1.   10,500
     x   11

2.   231
     x 32

3.   404
     x 12

4.   34,998
     x   12

Multiplying by Two Digits 4

Solve the multiplication problems.

1.   825
     x 63

2.   789
     x 45

3.   450
     x 63

4.   640
     x 96

Multiplication

Multiplying by Two Digits 5

Rewrite the problems in a vertical format and solve.

1. 255 x 99 =

2. 34,998 x 64 =

3. 798 x 53 =

4. 123 x 15 =

Multiplying by Three Digits 1

Solve the multiplication problems.

1.   212
   x 134

2.   133
   x 117

3.   405
   x 555

Multiplying by Three Digits 2

Solve the multiplication problems.

1.   615
   x 188

2.   2,201
   x 319

3.   3,500
   x 459

Multiplication

Multiplying by Three Digits 3

Solve the multiplication problems.

1.   1,035
       x   299

2.   4,000
       x   327

3.   80,500
       x   300

Multiplying by Three Digits 4

Solve the multiplication problems.

1.   2,201
       x   505

2.   3,500
       x   252

3.   10,000
       x   689

Multiplying by Three Digits 5

Rewrite the problems in a vertical format and solve.

1. 765 x 453 =

2. 365 x 291 =

3. 789 x 123 =

Multiplication

Multiplying Integers 1

When multiplying integers that include negative numbers, remember a few simple rules:

1) Two positive numbers multiplied result in a positive answer (product).
2) Two negative numbers multiplied result in a positive answer.
3) A positive number multiplied by a negative number results in a negative answer.

1. $8 \times -9 =$ ___   2. $6 \times 6 =$ ___
3. $-2 \times -20 =$ ___   4. $-3 \times 7 =$ ___
5. $10 \times -24 =$ ___   6. $4 \times -3 =$ ___

Multiplying Integers 2

Solve the multiplication problems. Be sure to place the correct sign in the answer.

1. $-13 \times 7 =$ _____

2. $-25 \times -15 =$ _____

3. $8 \times -12 =$ _____

4. $-2 \times -6 =$ _____

5. $4 \times 18 =$ _____

6. $42 \times -3 =$ _____

Multiplying Integers 3

Solve the multiplication problems. Be sure to place the correct sign in the answer.

1. $\begin{array}{r} -722 \\ \times \quad 4 \\ \hline \end{array}$ 2. $\begin{array}{r} 85 \\ \times -32 \\ \hline \end{array}$

3. $\begin{array}{r} -316 \\ \times \ -51 \\ \hline \end{array}$ 4. $\begin{array}{r} -407 \\ \times \quad -8 \\ \hline \end{array}$

Multiplying Integers 4

Solve the multiplication problems. Be sure to place the correct sign in the answer.

1. $\begin{array}{r} 625 \\ \times -214 \\ \hline \end{array}$ 2. $\begin{array}{r} -12 \\ \times -45 \\ \hline \end{array}$

3. $\begin{array}{r} -905 \\ \times \quad 10 \\ \hline \end{array}$ 4. $\begin{array}{r} -278 \\ \times \ -16 \\ \hline \end{array}$

Multiplication

Multiplying by 100, 1,000, or More 1

When a number is multiplied by 100, it is expanded by two decimal places, and two zeros are added to the end of the answer. For example, 225 x 100 becomes 22,500. The same pattern is continued for larger numbers such as 10,000 or 100,000. Solve the following problems quickly by inspection without going through all the steps of multiplication.

1. 75 x 100 = _____

2. 451 x 1,000 = _____

3. 1,542 x 10,000 = _____

Multiplying by 100, 1,000, or More 2

Solve the following problems quickly by inspection.

1. 100 x 34 = _____

2. 100 x 255 = _____

3. 515 x 100 = _____

4. 1,000 x 885 = _____

5. 10,000 x 65 = _____

6. 375 x 10,000 = _____

7. 10,000 x 1,000 = _____

Multiplying by 100, 1,000, or More 3

Vertical problems are easiest to solve with the multiple of 10 on the bottom. Solve the following problems quickly by inspection.

1.   65
    x 100

2.   350
    x   10

3.   785
    x 100

4.   525
    x 100

Multiplying by 100, 1,000, or More 4

Solve the following problems quickly by inspection.

1.   955
    x 1,000

2.   1,500
    x 1,000

3.   350
    x 1,000

4.   25
    x 10,000

Multiplication

Multiplying by 100, 1,000, or More 5

Solve the following problems quickly by inspection.

1.   650
       x 10,000

2.   2,000
       x 10,000

3.   75
       x 1,000

4.   200
       x 100,000

Multiplying With Decimals 1

Count the number of digits to the right of the decimal place in the factors. Then insert the decimal point that number of places to the left in the answer. For example, $4.9 \times 8.2 = 40.18$. Solve the multiplication problems.

1.   180
      x 2.2

2.   669
      x 10.3

3.   1,450
      x 4.55

4.   100.2
      x   80

Multiplying With Decimals 2

Solve the multiplication problems.

1.   2,500
      x 2.44

2.   7,422
      x   1.8

3.   340.88
      x   2.6

4.   15.75
      x   40

Multiplying With Decimals 3

Solve the multiplication problems.

1.   3,450
      x 2.55

2.   7,850
      x 2.95

3.   14,500
      x 0.752

4.   105.67
      x   95

Multiplication

Multiplying With Decimals 4

Solve the multiplication problems.

1.   375.82
   x   4.2

2.   17.5
   x   25

3.   1.35
   x   1.2

4.   62.5
   x 13.75

Multiplying With Decimals 5

Solve the multiplication problems.

1.   72,805
   x   2.2

2.   0.495
   x   0.17

3.   505
   x   1.4

4.   6.63
   x   0.3

Multiplying a Fraction by a Fraction 1

To multiply fractions, first multiply the **numerators**, or the top numbers. Then multiply the **denominators**, or the bottom numbers. If possible, simplify the answer. **Simplify** means to rewrite the answer in its lowest terms.

For example, $\dfrac{3}{4} \times \dfrac{2}{3} = \dfrac{3 \times 2}{4 \times 3} = \dfrac{6}{12} = \dfrac{1}{2}$

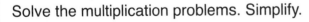
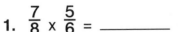

Solve the multiplication problems. Simplify.

1. $\dfrac{7}{8} \times \dfrac{5}{6} =$ _____

2. $\dfrac{5}{6} \times \dfrac{1}{12} =$ _____

3. $\dfrac{4}{5} \times \dfrac{1}{2} =$ _____

4. $\dfrac{3}{5} \times \dfrac{2}{3} =$ _____

5. $\dfrac{3}{8} \times \dfrac{3}{4} =$ _____

6. $\dfrac{2}{5} \times \dfrac{7}{10} =$ _____

Multiplication

Multiplying a Fraction by a Fraction 2

Solve the multiplication problems. Simplify.

1. $\frac{3}{5} \times \frac{3}{10}$ = _____

2. $\frac{4}{5} \times \frac{5}{6}$ = _____

3. $\frac{3}{5} \times \frac{7}{8}$ = _____

4. $\frac{5}{6} \times \frac{3}{10}$ = _____

Multiplying a Fraction by a Fraction 3

Solve the multiplication problems. Simplify.

1. $\frac{7}{8} \times \frac{4}{5}$ = _____

2. $\frac{3}{5} \times \frac{7}{10}$ = _____

3. $\frac{5}{8} \times \frac{3}{4}$ = _____

4. $\frac{3}{8} \times \frac{1}{2}$ = _____

Multiplying a Fraction by a Fraction 4

Solve the multiplication problems. Simplify.

1. $\frac{4}{5} \times \frac{2}{5}$ = _____

2. $\frac{4}{5} \times \frac{2}{3}$ = _____

3. $\frac{1}{3} \times \frac{1}{2}$ = _____

4. $\frac{2}{4} \times \frac{2}{3} \times \frac{1}{2}$ = _____

Multiplying a Fraction by a Fraction 5

Solve the multiplication problems. Simplify.

1. $\frac{3}{8} \times \frac{7}{10}$ = _____

2. $\frac{3}{4} \times \frac{6}{8}$ = _____

3. $\frac{9}{14} \times \frac{7}{9}$ = _____

4. $\frac{5}{6} \times \frac{1}{3} \times \frac{4}{5}$ = _____

Multiplication

Multiplying Fractions & Whole Numbers 1

To multiply fractions and whole numbers, first rewrite the whole number as a fraction by placing the whole number over the number 1. Next, multiply the **numerators**, or the top numbers. Then multiply the **denominators**, or the bottom numbers. If possible, simplify the answer. **Simplify** means to rewrite the answer in its lowest terms.

For example, $\dfrac{1}{2} \times 8 = \dfrac{1}{2} \times \dfrac{8}{1} = \dfrac{1 \times 8}{2 \times 1} = \dfrac{8}{2} = 4$

Solve the multiplication problems. Simplify.

1. $\dfrac{1}{8} \times 8 =$ _____

2. $19 \times \dfrac{3}{5} =$ _____

3. $\dfrac{1}{2} \times 23 =$ _____

4. $11 \times \dfrac{5}{6} =$ _____

Multiplying Fractions & Whole Numbers 2

Solve the multiplication problems. Simplify.

1. $5 \times \dfrac{1}{10} =$ _____

2. $\dfrac{1}{4} \times 31 =$ _____

3. $16 \times \dfrac{2}{3} =$ _____

4. $\dfrac{1}{8} \times 12 =$ _____

Multiplying Fractions & Whole Numbers 3

Solve the multiplication problems. Simplify.

1. $\dfrac{1}{3} \times 17 =$ _____

2. $25 \times \dfrac{1}{5} =$ _____

3. $6 \times \dfrac{3}{4} =$ _____

4. $\dfrac{7}{8} \times 14 =$ _____

Multiplication

Multiplying Fractions & Whole Numbers 4

Solve the multiplication problems. Simplify.

1. $12 \times \dfrac{7}{8} = $ _____

2. $\dfrac{3}{10} \times 21 = $ _____

3. $\dfrac{1}{6} \times 3 = $ _____

4. $35 \times \dfrac{4}{5} = $ _____

Multiplying Fractions & Whole Numbers 5

Solve the multiplication problems. Simplify.

1. $\dfrac{1}{4} \times 12 = $ _____

2. $7 \times \dfrac{2}{5} = $ _____

3. $\dfrac{2}{6} \times 24 \times \dfrac{3}{8} = $ _____

4. $\dfrac{1}{4} \times 5 \times \dfrac{4}{9} = $ _____

Multiplying Mixed Numbers 1

To multiply mixed numbers, first convert the mixed numbers to improper fractions. If one of the numbers being multiplied is a whole number, rewrite the whole number as a fraction by placing the whole number over the number 1. Next, multiply the **numerators**. Then multiply the **denominators**. If possible, simplify the answer. **Simplify** means to rewrite the answer in its lowest terms.

For example, $3\dfrac{1}{2} \times 2\dfrac{1}{2} = \dfrac{7}{2} \times \dfrac{5}{2} = \dfrac{7 \times 5}{2 \times 2} = \dfrac{35}{4} = 8\dfrac{3}{4}$

Solve the multiplication problems. Simplify.

1. $5\dfrac{5}{6} \times 2\dfrac{1}{7} = $ _____

2. $3\dfrac{1}{5} \times 6\dfrac{1}{4} = $ _____

3. $4\dfrac{4}{5} \times 3\dfrac{1}{8} = $ _____

4. $1\dfrac{4}{5} \times 6\dfrac{7}{8} = $ _____

Multiplication

Multiplying Mixed Numbers 2

Solve the multiplication problems. Simplify.

1. $1\frac{2}{3} \times 2\frac{1}{3} =$ _____

2. $3\frac{1}{2} \times 3\frac{1}{2} =$ _____

3. $1\frac{3}{5} \times 2\frac{1}{4} =$ _____

4. $2\frac{1}{7} \times 5\frac{1}{4} =$ _____

Multiplying Mixed Numbers 3

Solve the multiplication problems. Simplify.

1. $2\frac{1}{2} \times 2\frac{2}{5} =$ _____

2. $5\frac{5}{9} \times 2\frac{1}{4} =$ _____

3. $3\frac{1}{2} \times 2\frac{1}{4} =$ _____

4. $5\frac{1}{3} \times 3\frac{1}{8} =$ _____

Multiplying Mixed Numbers 4

Solve the multiplication problems. Simplify.

1. $1\frac{2}{3} \times 2\frac{1}{6} =$ _____

2. $3\frac{1}{2} \times 1\frac{1}{7} =$ _____

3. $2\frac{1}{10} \times 4\frac{2}{7} =$ _____

4. $1\frac{1}{8} \times 3\frac{2}{3} =$ _____

Multiplying Mixed Numbers 5

Solve the multiplication problems. Simplify.

1. $4\frac{1}{5} \times 2 =$ _____

2. $8\frac{2}{3} \times 1\frac{1}{2} =$ _____

3. $2\frac{7}{10} \times 6\frac{3}{12} =$ _____

4. $18 \times 3\frac{2}{5} =$ _____

Multiplication

Multiplying Fractions & Mixed Numbers: A Shortcut 1

Anytime you are multiplying fractions and/or mixed numbers, you can cross-cancel to make the problem easier to work with. Instead of simplifying the fraction at the end of the problem, you can **cross-cancel**, or simplify before you multiply.

For example, $3\frac{1}{8} \times 4\frac{4}{5} = \frac{25}{8} \times \frac{24}{5} = \frac{\overset{5}{\cancel{25}}}{\cancel{8}} \times \frac{\overset{3}{\cancel{24}}}{\cancel{5}} = \frac{15}{1} = 15$

Solve the multiplication problems. Cross-cancel if possible.

1. $\frac{4}{5} \times \frac{3}{8} =$ _____

2. $\frac{2}{5} \times 2\frac{3}{4} =$ _____

3. $\frac{4}{9} \times \frac{1}{2} =$ _____

4. $1\frac{4}{5} \times \frac{5}{6} =$ _____

5. $3\frac{1}{2} \times \frac{6}{7} =$ _____

6. $\frac{5}{8} \times \frac{3}{10} =$ _____

Multiplying Fractions & Mixed Numbers: A Shortcut 2

Solve the multiplication problems. Cross-cancel if possible.

1. $\frac{7}{9} \times \frac{3}{5} =$ _____

2. $6\frac{1}{4} \times \frac{2}{5} =$ _____

3. $3\frac{1}{5} \times \frac{1}{4} =$ _____

4. $\frac{5}{16} \times \frac{8}{9} =$ _____

Multiplying Fractions & Mixed Numbers: A Shortcut 3

Solve the multiplication problems. Cross-cancel if possible.

1. $\frac{6}{7} \times \frac{7}{8} =$ _____

2. $\frac{4}{5} \times \frac{7}{12} =$ _____

3. $1\frac{5}{9} \times \frac{3}{5} =$ _____

4. $\frac{3}{16} \times 5\frac{1}{3} =$ _____

Multiplication

Multiplication Review 1

1.	21 x 5	2.	36 x 3	3.	41 x 6

4.	70 x 8	5.	57 x 7	6.	98 x 4

66
x8
528

19.00
x4
76.00

126
X31
3906

Multiplication Review 2

Write the missing factors in the middle ring. The product is on the outside ring.

1.

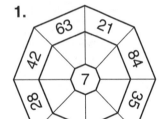

2.

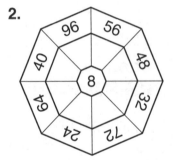

Multiplication Review 3

Compare the equations. Write >, <, or = on the blanks.

1. 3 x 4 _____ 6 x 4

2. 3 x 14 _____ 12 x 4

3. 7 x 7 _____ 5 x 9

4. 11 x 4 _____ 9 x 6

5. 4 x 12 _____ 6 x 8

6. 10 x 7 _____ 4 x 14

7. 14 x 3 _____ 3 x 15

8. 2 x 36 _____ 8 x 9

Multiplication

Multiplication Review 4

1. 4 x 6 = _____

2. 7 x 8 = _____

3. 9 x 6 = _____

4. 7 x 5 = _____

5. 8 x 8 = _____

6. 6 x 11 = _____

7. 4 x 12 = _____

8. 10 x 20 = _____

Multiplication Review 5

1. $\begin{array}{r} 14 \\ \times\ 41 \\ \hline \end{array}$

2. $\begin{array}{r} 46 \\ \times\ 64 \\ \hline \end{array}$

3. $\begin{array}{r} 72 \\ \times\ 27 \\ \hline \end{array}$

4. $\begin{array}{r} 44 \\ \times\ 44 \\ \hline \end{array}$

Multiplication Review 6

1. $\frac{2}{3} \times \frac{1}{3} =$ _____

2. $\frac{1}{4} \times \frac{3}{7} =$ _____

3. $\frac{2}{9} \times \frac{5}{8} =$ _____

4. $\frac{1}{12} \times \frac{1}{4} =$ _____

5. $\frac{2}{16} \times \frac{1}{9} =$ _____

6. $\frac{3}{8} \times \frac{5}{7} =$ _____

Multiplication Review 7

1. 3.7 x 4.9 = _____

2. 2.9 x 11.4 = _____

3. 7.3 x 4.7 = _____

3. 29.8 x 0.4 = _____

3. 792.45 x 32.1 = _____

3. 2,805.6 x 92.3 = _____

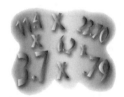

Division

Dividing Made Easier: Factors 1

Factors are the numbers that, when multiplied, result in a product. The factors of 16 are: 1, 2, 4, 8, 16. A **composite number**, such as 16, will have factors besides just 1 and itself. A **prime number** has only 1 and itself as factors. The numbers 11, 13, and 17 are examples of the many prime numbers.

List all factors for each number. Write "prime" if the number has only 1 and itself as factors.

1. 12 _____

2. 32 _____

Dividing Made Easier: Factors 2

List all factors for each number. Write "prime" if the number has only 1 and itself as factors.

1. 45 _____

2. 61 _____

3. 83 _____

4. 100 _____

Dividing Made Easier: Factors 3

List all factors for each number. Write "prime" if the number has only 1 and itself as factors.

1. 120 _____

2. 15 _____

3. 62 _____

4. 57 _____

Division

Dividing Made Easier: Factors 4

For these larger numbers, name any two corresponding factors. For example, 20 x 25 are a set of factors for 500.

1. 260 _____

2. 400 _____

3. 1,200 _____

4. 2,500 _____

5. 4,000 _____

Dividing Made Easier: Factors 5

For these larger numbers, name any two corresponding factors. For example, 20 x 25 are a set of factors for 500.

1. 88 _____

2. 102 _____

3. 99 _____

4. 1,300 _____

5. 2,600 _____

Division Models 1

Use the model below to show $36 \div 6$. Circle the sets of 6.

How many sets of 6 are in 36? _____

✳ ✳ ✳ ✳ ✳ ✳ ✳ ✳ ✳ ✳ ✳ ✳

✳ ✳ ✳ ✳ ✳ ✳ ✳ ✳ ✳ ✳ ✳ ✳

✳ ✳ ✳ ✳ ✳ ✳ ✳ ✳ ✳ ✳ ✳ ✳

Division Models 2

Use the model below to show $15 \div 3$. Circle the sets of 3.

How many sets of 3 are in 15? _____

■ ■ ■

■ ■ ■

■ ■ ■

■ ■ ■

■ ■ ■

Division

Division Models 3

Use the model below to show 35 ÷ 10. Circle the sets of 10.

How many sets of 10 are in 35? ____

How many items are left over (the

remainder)? ____

Division Models 4

Use the model below to show 64 ÷ 12. Circle the sets of 12.

How many sets of 12 are in 64? ____

How many items are left over (the

remainder)? ____

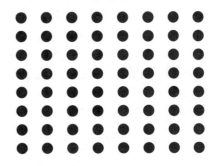

Dividing by Single Digits 1

Solve the division problems. Space has been left for checking your answer.

1. 4 $\overline{)404}$ **2.** 5 $\overline{)650}$

Check: Check:

Dividing by Single Digits 2

Solve the division problems. Space has been left for checking your answer.

1. 7 $\overline{)810}$ **2.** 8 $\overline{)704}$

Check: Check:

Division

Dividing by Single Digits 3

Solve the division problems. Space has been left for checking your answer.

1. $2\overline{)673}$ **2.** $9\overline{)599}$

Check: Check:

Dividing by Single Digits 4

Solve the division problems. Space has been left for checking your answer.

1. $2\overline{)650}$ **2.** $5\overline{)585}$

Check: Check:

Dividing by Single Digits 5

Rewrite in vertical form and solve.

1. $786 \div 3 =$ _____

2. $900 \div 4 =$ _____

3. $405 \div 5 =$ _____

Dividing by Single Digits 6

Rewrite in vertical form and solve.

1. $825 \div 4 =$ _____

2. $421 \div 3 =$ _____

3. $255 \div 2 =$ _____

Division

Remainders 1

The remainder is a leftover portion that won't divide out evenly. The remainder can be written as a fraction because it is a fractional portion.

For example, $207 \div 7 = 29 \text{ r } 4 = 29\frac{4}{7}$.

Solve each division problem. Write the remainders as fractions.

1. $9\,\overline{)499}$ **2.** $5\,\overline{)7,811}$

Remainders 2

Solve each division problem. Write the remainders as fractions.

1. $8\,\overline{)625}$ **2.** $4\,\overline{)133}$

3. $2\,\overline{)1,255}$ **4.** $6\,\overline{)555}$

Remainders 3

Solve each division problem. Write the remainders as fractions.

1. $3\,\overline{)378}$ **2.** $5\,\overline{)707}$

3. $8\,\overline{)675}$ **4.** $4\,\overline{)150}$

Remainders 4

Solve each division problem. Write the remainders as fractions.

1. $9\,\overline{)1,500}$ **2.** $3\,\overline{)525}$

3. $8\,\overline{)380}$ **4.** $6\,\overline{)8,100}$

Division

Remainders 5

Rewrite each problem in a vertical format and solve.
Write the remainders as fractions.

1. 500 ÷ 9 = _____

2. 7,915 ÷ 4 = _____

3. 650 ÷ 7 = _____

4. 1,300 ÷ 3 = _____

Dividing by Two Digits 1

Solve. For those with remainders, write the remainder as a fraction.

1. 13)615

2. 40)388

3. 75)642

Dividing by Two Digits 2

Solve. For those with remainders, write the remainder as a fraction.

1. 31)999

2. 90)6,155

3. 15)3,250

Division

Dividing by Two Digits 3

Solve. For those with remainders, write the remainder as a fraction.

1. $28 \overline{)26{,}624}$ **2.** $67 \overline{)60{,}750}$ **3.** $89 \overline{)16{,}800}$

Dividing by Two Digits 4

Solve. For those with remainders, write the remainder as a fraction.

1. $50 \overline{)50{,}000}$ **2.** $10 \overline{)2{,}500}$ **3.** $48 \overline{)128{,}000}$

Dividing by Two Digits 5

Solve. For those with remainders, write the remainder as a fraction.

1. $25 \overline{)678}$ **2.** $30 \overline{)26{,}650}$ **3.** $95 \overline{)6{,}150}$

Division

Dividing by 10 1

A number that is divided by 10 is reduced by one place value. For example, $900 \div 10 = 90$.

Solve by inspection.

1. $850 \div 10 =$ _____

2. $390 \div 10 =$ _____

3. $4,500 \div 10 =$ _____

4. $1,050 \div 10 =$ _____

5. $43,000 \div 10 =$ _____

Dividing by 10 2

A number that is divided by 10 is reduced by one place value. For example, $900 \div 10 = 90$.

Solve by inspection.

1. $12,300 \div 10 =$ _____

2. $920 \div 10 =$ _____

3. $830 \div 10 =$ _____

4. $7,200 \div 10 =$ _____

5. $65,500 \div 10 =$ _____

Dividing by 10 3

A number that is divided by 10 is reduced by one place value. For example, $900 \div 10 = 90$.

Solve by inspection.

1. $740 \div 10 =$ _____

2. $610 \div 10 =$ _____

3. $1,520 \div 10 =$ _____

4. $3,100 \div 10 =$ _____

5. $28,000 \div 10 =$ _____

Dividing by 10 4

A number that is divided by 10 is reduced by one place value. For example, $900 \div 10 = 90$.

Solve by inspection.

1. $500 \div 10 =$ _____

2. $480 \div 10 =$ _____

3. $6,430 \div 10 =$ _____

4. $29,710 \div 10 =$ _____

5. $525,900 \div 10 =$ _____

Division

Dividing by 100 or 1,000 1

A number that is divided by 100 or 1,000 is reduced by two or three place values. For example, 62,000 ÷ 100 = 620 or 62,000 ÷ 1,000 = 62.

Solve by inspection.

1. 3,000 ÷ 100 = _____

2. 50,000 ÷ 1,000 = _____

3. 1,200 ÷ 100 = _____

4. 8,800 ÷ 100 = _____

5. 15,000 ÷ 1,000 = _____

Dividing by 100 or 1,000 2

A number that is divided by 100 or 1,000 is reduced by two or three place values. For example, 62,000 ÷ 100 = 620 or 62,000 ÷ 1,000 = 62.

Solve by inspection.

1. 25,500 ÷ 100 = _____

2. 2,500 ÷ 100 = _____

3. 9,900 ÷ 100 = _____

4. 25,000 ÷ 1,000 = _____

5. 725,000 ÷ 1,000 = _____

Dividing by 100 or 1,000 3

A number that is divided by 100 or 1,000 is reduced by two or three place values. For example, 62,000 ÷ 100 = 620 or 62,000 ÷ 1,000 = 62.

Solve by inspection.

1. 4,000 ÷ 100 = _____

2. 5,600 ÷ 100 = _____

3. 30,000 ÷ 100 = _____

4. 45,000 ÷ 1,000 = _____

5. 178,000 ÷ 1,000 = _____

Dividing by 100 or 1,000 4

A number that is divided by 100 or 1,000 is reduced by two or three place values. For example, 62,000 ÷ 100 = 620 or 62,000 ÷ 1,000 = 62.

Solve by inspection.

1. 9,100 ÷ 100 = _____

2. 68,000 ÷ 100 = _____

3. 57,000 ÷ 1,000 = _____

4. 79,000 ÷ 1,000 = _____

5. 432,000 ÷ 1,000 = _____

Division

Dividing by Three Digits 1

Solve. For those with remainders, write the remainder as a fraction.

1. 125) 2,355   **2.** 344) 1,299   **3.** 188) 2,090

Dividing by Three Digits 2

Solve. For those with remainders, write the remainder as a fraction.

1. 900) 2,090   **2.** 375) 13,750   **3.** 100) 1,200

Dividing by Three Digits 3

Solve. For those with remainders, write the remainder as a fraction.

1. 899) 1,100   **2.** 641) 18,822   **3.** 705) 205,800

Division

Dividing by Three Digits 4

Solve. For those with remainders, write the remainder as a fraction.

1. $202\overline{)7,437}$ **2.** $512\overline{)14,168}$ **3.** $615\overline{)972,803}$

Dividing by Three Digits 5

Solve. For those with remainders, write the remainder as a fraction.

1. $333\overline{)64,209}$ **2.** $176\overline{)12,783}$ **3.** $224\overline{)175,389}$

Dividing Integers 1

Here are the rules for dividing with **integers** (signed numbers).

1) When dividing a posititve number by a positive number, the answer (**quotient**) is positive. 2) When dividing a positive number by a negative number or a negative number by a positive number, the answer is negative. 3) When dividing a negative number by a negative number, the answer is positive.

Solve these problems on your own paper. For those with remainders, write the remainder as a fraction. Be sure to write the correct sign in the answer.

1. $-25\overline{)1,050}$ **2.** $234\overline{)-89,636}$ **3.** $-8\overline{)-6,429}$

Division

Dividing Integers 2

Solve. For those with remainders, write the remainder as a fraction. Be sure to write the correct sign in the answer.

1. 4)-2,516

2. -17)72,899

3. -414)-821,950

Dividing Integers 3

Solve. For those with remainders, write the remainder as a fraction. Be sure to write the correct sign in the answer.

1. -44)72,156

2. 9)62,387

3. 65)-32,147

Dividing Integers 4

Solve. For those with remainders, write the remainder as a fraction. Be sure to write the correct sign in the answer.

1. -112)-402,695

2. -82)243

3. 91)-27,432

Division

Dividing Integers 5

Quickly solve by inspection. Be sure to write the correct sign in the answer.

1. $24 \div -6 =$ _____

2. $-18 \div -9 =$ _____

3. $36 \div -4 =$ _____

4. $-12 \div -6 =$ _____

5. $32 \div 8 =$ _____

6. $48 \div -8 =$ _____

Dividing Integers 6

Quickly solve by inspection. Be sure to write the correct sign in the answer.

1. $-35 \div -5 =$ _____

2. $9 \div -3 =$ _____

3. $14 \div 2 =$ _____

4. $-44 \div 11 =$ _____

5. $-27 \div 9 =$ _____

6. $-21 \div -7 =$ _____

Converting Fractions to Decimals 1

You can convert a fractional remainder to a decimal by dividing the top number (**numerator**) by the bottom number (**denominator**).

For example, $1{,}024 \div 28 = 36 \frac{16}{28}$. $16 \div 28 = 0.5714285$. Add this to 36, so the answer is 36.5714285. Answers are usually rounded to the fourth decimal place.

Convert these fractions to decimals. You may use a calculator. Round to the fourth decimal place.

1. $\frac{5}{6}$ _____   2. $\frac{17}{30}$ _____   3. $\frac{1}{25}$ _____

4. $\frac{9}{20}$ _____   5. $\frac{24}{25}$ _____   6. $\frac{645}{710}$ _____

Division

Converting Fractions to Decimals 2

Convert these fractions to decimals. You may use a calculator. Round to the fourth decimal place.

1. $\dfrac{7}{8}$ _____

2. $\dfrac{1}{14}$ _____

3. $\dfrac{2}{3}$ _____

4. $\dfrac{11}{12}$ _____

5. $\dfrac{7}{26}$ _____

Converting Fractions to Decimals 3

Using a calculator, convert the whole numbers with fractional portions to decimal numbers. Express answers only to four places after the decimal.

1. $3\dfrac{3}{8} = 3.$_____

2. $10\dfrac{16}{19} = 10.$_____

3. $24\dfrac{34}{109} = 24.$_____

4. $59\dfrac{1}{9} = 59.$_____

5. $164\dfrac{202}{239} = 164.$_____

Converting Fractions to Decimals 4

Using a calculator, convert the whole numbers with fractional portions to decimal numbers. Express answers only to four places after the decimal.

1. $185\dfrac{17}{40} = 185.$_____

2. $44\dfrac{9}{50} = 44.$_____

3. $16\dfrac{7}{8} = 16.$_____

4. $194\dfrac{34}{40} = 194.$_____

5. $5\dfrac{663}{665} = 5.$_____

Converting Fractions to Decimals 5

Using a calculator, convert the whole numbers with fractional portions to decimal numbers. Express answers only to four places after the decimal.

1. $7\dfrac{8}{10} = 7.$_____

2. $10\dfrac{5}{20} = 10.$_____

3. $25\dfrac{25}{110} = 25.$_____

4. $190\dfrac{20}{35} = 190.$_____

5. $16\dfrac{19}{20} = 16.$_____

Division

Dividing With Decimals 1

When dividing with decimals, first make the divisor a whole number by moving the decimal point to the right as many places as necessary. Then move the decimal point in the dividend that same number of places.

For example, $7.5 \overline{)225}$ becomes $75. \overline{)2250}$.

Solve by first making the divisor a whole number.

1. $5.5 \overline{)396}$ **2.** $4.8 \overline{)196.8}$ **3.** $3.2 \overline{)345.6}$

Dividing With Decimals 2

Solve by first making the divisor a whole number.

1. $1.25 \overline{)77.5}$

2. $10.8 \overline{)950.4}$

Dividing With Decimals 3

Solve by first making the divisor a whole number.

1. $6.45 \overline{)483.75}$

2. $22.6 \overline{)406.8}$

$64.2 \overline{)2472}$

$5.25 \overline{)775}$ $.39 \overline{)936.5}$

Division

Dividing With Decimals 4

Solve by first making the divisor a whole number.

1. $20.25 \overline{)810}$

2. $14.88 \overline{)2{,}023.68}$

Dividing With Decimals 5

Solve by first making the divisor a whole number.

1. $120.4 \overline{)22{,}033.2}$

2. $5.6 \overline{)397.6}$

Dividing With Decimals 6

Solve by first making the divisor a whole number.

1. $3.5 \overline{)350.35}$

2. $15.75 \overline{)2{,}025.45}$

Dividing With Decimals 7

Solve by first making the divisor a whole number.

1. $6.35 \overline{)488.95}$

2. $125.5 \overline{)24{,}974.5}$

Division

Dividing With Fractions: Reciprocals 1

One number is the **reciprocal** of another if their product is 1. The reciprocal of a fraction is obtained by **inverting** the fraction, or by flipping the **numerator** (top number) and the **denominator** (bottom number). The reciprocal of a whole number is found by placing the whole number over a denominator of 1, then inverting to get the fraction.

Examples: The reciprocal of $\frac{3}{4}$ is $\frac{4}{3}$. The reciprocal of 4 is $\frac{1}{4}$.

The reciprocal of $2\frac{1}{2}$ is $\frac{2}{5}$.

Find the reciprocal of each fraction, whole number, or mixed number below.

1. $\frac{3}{7}$ _____

2. $1\frac{1}{4}$ _____

3. $\frac{7}{8}$ _____

4. 7 _____

Dividing With Fractions: Reciprocals 2

Find the reciprocal of each fraction, whole number, or mixed number below.

1. $9\frac{3}{4}$ _____

2. 21 _____

3. $\frac{5}{6}$ _____

4. $14\frac{1}{2}$ _____

5. $\frac{4}{5}$ _____

6. $9\frac{3}{5}$ _____

Dividing With Fractions: Reciprocals 3

Find the reciprocal of each fraction, whole number, or mixed number below.

1. $\frac{2}{3}$ _____

2. 73 _____

3. 5 _____

4. $5\frac{1}{6}$ _____

5. $\frac{1}{12}$ _____

6. $10\frac{1}{3}$ _____

Division

Dividing by Fractions 1

When dividing a fraction by a fraction, first invert the second fraction. This fraction is now a reciprocal. Change the division sign to a multiplication sign. Multiply the two fractions. If possible, simplify the answer.

Example: $\dfrac{2}{3} \div \dfrac{1}{6} = \dfrac{2}{3} \times \dfrac{6}{1} = \dfrac{2 \times 6}{3 \times 1} = \dfrac{12}{3} = 4$

Solve the problems below by dividing the fractions. Simplify the answers.

1. $\dfrac{8}{9} \div \dfrac{1}{3} =$ _____

2. $\dfrac{5}{12} \div \dfrac{2}{3} =$ _____

3. $\dfrac{6}{7} \div \dfrac{2}{3} =$ _____

4. $\dfrac{3}{5} \div \dfrac{7}{8} =$ _____

Dividing by Fractions 2

Solve the problems below by dividing the fractions. Simplify the answers.

1. $\dfrac{9}{10} \div \dfrac{1}{2} =$ _____

2. $\dfrac{3}{5} \div \dfrac{5}{6} =$ _____

3. $\dfrac{3}{4} \div \dfrac{2}{5} =$ _____

4. $\dfrac{1}{2} \div \dfrac{1}{8} =$ _____

Dividing by Fractions 3

Solve the problems below by dividing the fractions. Simplify the answers.

1. $\dfrac{2}{9} \div \dfrac{3}{12} =$ _____

2. $\dfrac{1}{12} \div \dfrac{3}{15} =$ _____

3. $\dfrac{3}{8} \div \dfrac{4}{5} =$ _____

4. $\dfrac{1}{15} \div \dfrac{3}{15} =$ _____

Division

Dividing by Fractions 4

Solve the problems below by dividing the fractions. Simplify the answers.

1. $\dfrac{5}{6} \div \dfrac{5}{6} =$ _____

2. $\dfrac{3}{20} \div \dfrac{3}{5} =$ _____

3. $\dfrac{3}{10} \div \dfrac{4}{5} =$ _____

4. $\dfrac{1}{8} \div \dfrac{5}{6} =$ _____

Dividing by Fractions 5

Solve the problems below by dividing the fractions. Simplify the answers.

1. $\dfrac{1}{4} \div \dfrac{1}{3} =$ _____

2. $\dfrac{1}{2} \div \dfrac{2}{5} =$ _____

3. $\dfrac{7}{8} \div \dfrac{1}{14} =$ _____

4. $\dfrac{10}{12} \div \dfrac{6}{9} =$ _____

Dividing Whole Numbers & Mixed Numbers 1

When dividing whole numbers and/or mixed numbers, place whole numbers over a denominator of 1. Convert mixed numbers to improper fractions. Invert the second number (**divisor**) and change the sign to multiplication. Convert the answer back to a mixed number, whole number, or simplified fraction.

Example: $14 \div 2\dfrac{1}{2} = \dfrac{14}{1} \div \dfrac{5}{2} = \dfrac{14}{1} \times \dfrac{2}{5} = \dfrac{28}{5} = 5\dfrac{3}{5}$

Solve the problems below by dividing the whole numbers and mixed numbers. Simplify the answers.

1. $8 \div 1\dfrac{3}{5} =$ _____

2. $18 \div 1\dfrac{4}{5} =$ _____

3. $2\dfrac{1}{2} \div 8 =$ _____

4. $2\dfrac{1}{4} \div 2\dfrac{1}{2} =$ _____

Division

Dividing Whole Numbers & Mixed Numbers 2

Solve the problems below by dividing the whole numbers and mixed numbers. Simplify the answers.

1. $3\frac{3}{8} \div 9 =$ _____

2. $4\frac{1}{6} \div 1\frac{1}{3} =$ _____

3. $7 \div 3\frac{1}{2} =$ _____

4. $12 \div 2\frac{2}{3} =$ _____

Dividing Whole Numbers & Mixed Numbers 3

Solve the problems below by dividing the whole numbers and mixed numbers. Simplify the answers.

1. $4\frac{1}{2} \div 1\frac{1}{2} =$ _____

2. $1\frac{2}{7} \div 5 =$ _____

3. $2\frac{1}{4} \div 1\frac{3}{4} =$ _____

4. $5\frac{5}{6} \div 7 =$ _____

Dividing Whole Numbers & Mixed Numbers 4

Solve the problems below by dividing the whole numbers and mixed numbers. Simplify the answers.

1. $25 \div 3\frac{1}{8} =$ _____

2. $7\frac{1}{5} \div 1\frac{1}{5} =$ _____

3. $3\frac{1}{8} \div 4\frac{1}{2} =$ _____

4. $36 \div 1\frac{1}{2} =$ _____

Dividing Whole Numbers & Mixed Numbers 5

Solve the problems below by dividing the whole numbers and mixed numbers. Simplify the answers.

1. $4 \div 1\frac{1}{2} =$ _____

2. $5\frac{1}{4} \div 1\frac{3}{4} =$ _____

3. $7 \div \frac{2}{5} =$ _____

4. $1\frac{2}{3} \div 2\frac{1}{4} =$ _____

Division

Division Review 1

Complete the division facts charts. Divide each number in the left column by the number at the top of the chart.

1.

÷	5
15	3
35	
75	
90	
30	

2.

÷	6
42	
36	
54	
72	
24	

3.

÷	7
49	
42	
56	
28	
77	

4.

÷	8
56	
64	
24	
32	
72	

Division Review 2

Double-check your answers by multiplying.

1. $6\overline{)528}$ **2.** $7\overline{)455}$ **3.** $12\overline{)1,368}$

$\underline{\times\ 6}$ $\underline{\times\ 7}$ $\underline{\times\ 12}$

Division Review 3

Complete the chart.

1. 9 x ____ = 63

63 ÷ 9 = ____

____ x 9 = 63

63 ÷ ____ = 9

2. 8 x ____ = 56

56 ÷ 8 = ____

____ x 8 = 56

56 ÷ ____ = 8

3. 7 x ____ = 42

42 ÷ 7 = ____

____ x 7 = 42

42 ÷ ____ = 7

Division

Division Review 4

1. $81 \div 9 =$ _____

2. $63 \div 7 =$ _____

3. $56 \div 7 =$ _____

4. $42 \div 6 =$ _____

5. $48 \div 12 =$ _____

6. $54 \div 9 =$ _____

Division Review 5

Write the remainder as a whole number.

1. $83 \div 7 =$ ____R____

2. $99 \div 8 =$ ____R____

3. $36 \div 11 =$ ____R____

4. $76 \div 3 =$ ____R____

5. $51 \div 6 =$ ____R____

6. $54 \div 5 =$ ____R____

Division Review 6

1. $\dfrac{1}{7} \div \dfrac{3}{7} =$ _____

2. $\dfrac{3}{9} \div \dfrac{2}{9} =$ _____

3. $\dfrac{4}{5} \div \dfrac{2}{5} =$ _____

4. $\dfrac{1}{8} \div 7 =$ _____

5. $2\dfrac{6}{7} \div 4\dfrac{1}{2} =$ _____

Division Review 7

Solve. Round quotients to the nearest hundredth if necessary.

1. $16.92 \div 4.7 =$ _____

2. $22.68 \div 6.3 =$ _____

3. $104.78 \div 12.2 =$ _____

4. $1{,}735.26 \div 99.07 =$ _____

5. $21{,}698 \div 42.6 =$ _____

6. $35{,}603.1 \div 3.22 =$ _____

Multiplication & Division Word Problems

Multiplication Word Problems 1

1. Jerry, Terry, and Merry each have $17. How much do they have all together? _____

2. Harry, Larry, and Kerry each jogged 36 miles last week. How many miles all together? _____

3. Holly, Dolly, and Polly each picked 84 quarts of strawberries. How many quarts all together? _____

Multiplication Word Problems 2

1. 3 monkeys: each has 4 bananas. How many bananas? _____

2. 7 pigs: each pig wears 3 pink bows. How many bows? _____

3. 4 baby giraffes: each giraffe has 28 spots. How many spots? _____

Multiplication Word Problems 3

1. 7 toddlers: 32 toys each. How many toys all together? _____

2. 11 leopards: 79 spots each. How many spots in all? _____

3. 9 boxes of discs: 35 discs in each box. How many discs in all? _____

4. 8 helpings of real mashed potatoes: 14 lumps in each helping. How many lumps in all? _____

Multiplication & Division Word Problems

Multiplication Word Problems 4

1. 9 cases of widgets: each case weighs 125 pounds. How many pounds in all? _____

2. 9 cases of widgets: each case contains 200 widgets. How many widgets? _____

Multiplication Word Problems 5

1. Jessie bought five packages of radish seeds at 23¢ each. How much did she spend on radish seeds? _____

2. Jessie bought four yellow rose bushes for $3.99 each. How much did she spend on rose bushes? _____

3. Jessie ordered eight tons of pea gravel at $17.23 per ton. How much did Jessie spend on pea gravel? _____

Multiplication Word Problems 6

Rob's Rental Rates

circus tent	$73/day	juggler	$19/hour
lion tamer	$73/hour	clown	$27/hour
lion	$114/hour	elephant	$125/hour

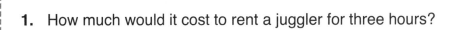

1. How much would it cost to rent a juggler for three hours?

   _____

2. How much would it cost to rent a circus tent for four days? _____

3. How much would it cost to rent a clown for six hours? _____

4. How much would it cost to rent a lion tamer and three lions for two hours?

   _____

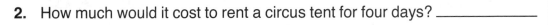

Multiplication & Division Word Problems

Multiplication Word Problems 7

Crystal Cave had 186 visitors an hour for six hours on Monday. Admission is $5.00 per adult and $3.00 per child. Half the visitors on Monday were adults and half were children.

1. How many visitors went to Crystal Cave on Monday? _____

2. How much did Crystal Cave earn in adult admission fees on Monday?

   _____

3. How much in child admission fees? _____

4. Each visitor spent an average of $4.00 in the cafeteria on Monday. How much did visitors spend in the cafeteria? _____

Multiplication Word Problems 8

1. Lisa has three quarters, five dimes, seven nickels, and 12 pennies. How much money does she have in all? _____

2. Jim has five quarters, 12 dimes, four nickels, and 28 pennies. How much money does he have all together? _____

3. Josh has two half dollars, 12 quarters, four dimes, and 16 nickels. How much money does Josh have? _____

Multiplication Word Problems 9

1. Melissa jogged 3.7 miles a day for 7 days. How far did she jog in all? _____

2. The Hungry Lion Cafe served 9.5 pies a day for 30 days. How many pies did they serve in all? _____

Multiplication & Division Word Problems

Multiplication Word Problems 10

1. Five delivery trucks have been loaded with 15,000 pounds of packages each. How many pounds will be delivered once all five trucks have delivered their loads?

   _____

2. Water rushes out of a water slide at a rate of 120 gallons a minute. How many gallons will rush out in 10 hours?

   _____

Multiplication Word Problems 11

1. Kathy's cookie recipe calls for $\frac{2}{3}$ cup of sugar. How much sugar would she use to make $\frac{2}{3}$ of a batch of cookies? _____

2. On Saturday, Nick picked 10 bushels of apples. Monday, Shane picked $\frac{1}{3}$ as many apples as Nick. How many bushels of apples did Shane pick on Monday? _____

Multiplication Word Problems 12

1. Last week, Joslyn walked $3\frac{1}{2}$ miles. This week, she plans on walking $1\frac{1}{5}$ times as far as last week. How many miles does Joslyn plan on walking this week? _____

2. Mona's Cookie Shack sold $\frac{2}{3}$ as many chocolate chip cookies as sugar cookies. If they sold 3 trays of sugar cookies, how many trays of chocolate chip cookies did they sell? _____

Multiplication Word Problems 13

1. A tomato that weighed $3\frac{1}{4}$ pounds won the contest at the fair. How many ounces did it weigh? _____

2. Steak is priced at $7.50 a pound. What would be the price of a steak that weighs $1\frac{1}{8}$ pounds?

   _____

Multiplication & Division Word Problems

Division Word Problems 1

1. 48 mice divided into 4 equal groups. How many in each group? _____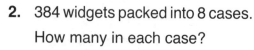

2. 384 widgets packed into 8 cases. How many in each case?

   _____

3. 621 chocolate stars packed into 9 bags. How many in each bag?

   _____

4. 238 pounds of cheese cut into 8-ounce blocks. How many blocks of cheese? _____

Division Word Problems 2

1. Jenny read 22 pages of a novel each day. How many days did it take her to finish a 264-page novel? _____

2. Brenda blew up 17 helium balloons in 35 minutes. How many balloons did she blow up in an hour and 45 minutes? _____

3. Carlos took 126 photos while on vacation. He arranged the photos in an album with six photos per page. How many pages did he fill with his vacation photos? _____

Division Word Problems 3

List eight ways to divide 80 objects with an even number of objects in each group. For example, one way would be 10 groups with 8 objects in each group.

1. _____ groups, _____ in each group

2. _____ groups, _____ in each group

3. _____ groups, _____ in each group

4. _____ groups, _____ in each group

5. _____ groups, _____ in each group

6. _____ groups, _____ in each group

7. _____ groups, _____ in each group

8. _____ groups, _____ in each group

Multiplication & Division Word Problems

Division Word Problems 4

1. Jacob drove 468 miles in 9 hours. On the average, how many miles did he drive per hour?

   _____

2. Six cafeteria workers dished out 645 bowls of mustard and chocolate chip soup. On the average, how many bowls did each worker dish out?

   _____

Division Word Problems 5

The school librarian kept track of the number of students using the Internet each day for a week:

Mon.: 57   Tues.: 39   Wed.: 76
Thu.: 87   Fri.: 91

On the average, how many students used the Internet each day?

_____

Division Word Problems 6

1. Toby used 8.7 gallons of gas to drive 478 miles. How many miles per gallon did he get? Round your answer to the nearest tenth.

   _____

2. Tony spent $23.70 on ice cream bars in June. Ice cream bars cost 79¢ each. How many did he buy?

   _____

Division Word Problems 7

1. After Mr. Smith passed away and all the expenses were paid, his estate was valued at $234,000. This amount will be split equally among his 52 surviving heirs. How much money will each heir receive?

   _____

2. In a recent fundraiser for a charity, $4,340 was collected by 31 different volunteers. On average, how much money did each volunteer collect?

   _____

Multiplication & Division Word Problems

Division Word Problems 8

1. An error caused 34,500 parts to be packaged incorrectly. If it took the workers 23 days to repackage the parts correctly, how many parts did they repackage each day?

_____

2. A herd of 1,680 cattle are being sorted into 12 different pastures. How many animals should go to each pasture to keep the numbers equal in each location?

_____

Division Word Problems 9

1. Adam used three thousand, six hundred chips to make a big batch of giant chocolate chip cookies. Each cookie got an average of sixteen chips. How many cookies did Adam make?

_____

2. Kayla computed that the distance she walked between home and school over seventeen days was a total of five thousand, two hundred thirty-six yards. About how far did she walk each day?

_____

Division Word Problems 10

1. A shipping company delivered eighty-two thousand, five hundred packages in North Dakota during the month of May. If there were two hundred fifteen delivery routes, how many packages were delivered on each route?

_____

2. Chicken Licken will open thirty new restaurants next year. They will need to hire one thousand twenty new employees. How many employees will each restaurant get?

_____

Multiplication & Division Word Problems

Division Word Problems 11

1. Darren has thirty action figures. He shares them equally among ten friends. How many action figures does each friend get?

    _____

2. Sarah has $4 in her purse. Each book in the used-book section costs $2. How many books can she buy?

    _____

Division Word Problems 12

1. There are twenty-seven soft drink machines in the college. They hold five hundred thirteen cases of soft drinks all together. How many cases does each machine hold?

    _____

2. There are four thousand, seven hundred twenty-five offices in that tall building. The building has 105 stories. How many offices does each story of the building have?

    _____

Division Word Problems 13

1. Randy wants to make a 20-foot path of stepping stones. Each stone is $\frac{10}{12}$ of a foot long. How many stepping stones will he need? _____

2. Flood water is rising at $1\frac{1}{2}$ inches per hour. How many hours will it take the water to rise 12 inches?

    _____

Division Word Problems 14

1. A bird feeder holds $\frac{1}{2}$ cup of bird-seed. The feeder is filled with a scoop that holds $\frac{1}{6}$ of a cup. How many scoops will be needed to fill the feeder? _____

2. A can of dog food is $22\frac{3}{4}$ ounces. Each can contains $3\frac{1}{2}$ servings. How many ounces are in a serving? _____

Multiplication & Division Word Problems

Mixed-Operation Word Problems 1

1. Emilio worked for 6 hours and earned $5 an hour at one part-time job. He earned a total of $24 at another job that paid $6 an hour. How many hours did Emilio work all together?

   _____

2. How much did Emilio earn all together? _____

Mixed-Operation Word Problems 2

1. Which is the better buy: two 12-ounce cans of tuna for $1.49 or one 8-ounce can for 79¢?

   _____

2. Which is the best buy: 6 pairs of socks for $6.99, 3 pairs for $3.99, or one pair for $1.13?

   _____

Mixed-Operation Word Problems 3

1. Liza is the cashier at the local grocery store. Her till ended with $2,831.59, and she served 25 patrons. What is the average amount each person spent? (Round to the nearest hundredth.) _____

2. Jacob bought 10 soft drinks for his friends. Each drink cost $1.25. How much did he pay for the drinks? _____

Mixed-Operation Word Problems 4

1. Tara is saving to buy a membership to the local amusement park. The membership fee is $41.50. If she has 10 weeks to save for it, how much money should she save every week?

   _____

2. Ron gets $0.04 for every paper he delivers. How much did he earn if he delivered 115 papers?

   _____

Multiplication & Division Word Problems

Mixed-Operation Word Problems 5

An easy way to check a division problem is to multiply the quotient by the divisor. If there is a remainder, add it to the product. The result should be the dividend.

When Jared organized his sports card collection, he realized he had duplicate cards. He decided to divide the 210 extra sports cards among five of his friends.

1. How many cards would each of his friends receive? _____

2. Before counting out the cards, Jared multiplied to be sure that he had divided them equally. Wrte the multiplication problem Jared used.

    _____

3. One of Jared's friends decided he did not want any cards, so Jared divided them into four sets instead. How many cards would be in each new set? How many would be left over? _____

4. Write the multiplication problem Jared used to check his division.

    _____

Mixed-Operation Word Problems 6

Jake and his family share a new computer. Friday night is Jake's turn. He has $1\frac{1}{4}$ hours after dinner to use the machine.

1. On his first Friday night, Jake sent e-mails to his friends. If each e-mail took $\frac{1}{8}$ hour to finish, how many e-mails did he send? _____

2. On his second Friday night, Jake played his favorite computer game. If each level took $\frac{1}{2}$ hour to finish, how many levels did he complete?

    _____

3. On his third Friday night, Jake wrote movie reviews for his blog. If each review took $\frac{1}{3}$ hour to finish, how many reviews did he write? _____

4. On his fourth Friday night, Jake chatted with friends. If he chatted with each friend for $\frac{1}{4}$ hour, how many friends did he contact? _____

Multiplication & Division Word Problems

Mixed-Operation Word Problems 7

Jeremy is delivering packages after school to earn extra money for the holidays. He has eight boxes of packages he needs to deliver during a five-day time period. There are sixteen packages in each box. If Jeremy wants to deliver about the same number of packages each day, approximately how many packages should Jeremy deliver after school each day during the five-day period?

_____

_____

Mixed-Operation Word Problems 8

Jason and Shane are both on the yearbook staff. They take 776 pictures for the yearbook during the school year. They can only use 138 pictures in the yearbook. The yearbook is 68 pages long. They plan to put the same number of pictures on each page. If they have any extra pictures, they will put them on the last page of the yearbook. How many pictures will Jason and Shane put on each regular page? How many pictures will they put on the last page?

_____

_____

Mixed-Operation Word Problems 9

Macy is dividing up cookies to sell at the school bake sale. She has a total of 878 cookies. She plans to place three cookies in each bag and sell each bag for $0.75. How many three-cookie bags can Macy make? How much money will she make if she sells all the bags?

_____

_____

Answer Keys

Multiplication Models 1 (p. 2)
1. 3; 8; 24   2. 4; 4; 16

Multiplication Models 2 (p. 2)
7; 6; 42

Multiplication Models 3 (p. 2)
1. 2; 12; 24   2. 5; 2; 10

Multiplication Models 4 (p. 2)
10; 7; 70

Multiplication Models 5 (p. 3)
Models will vary. Teacher check that the rows and columns equal 48.

Multiples 1 (p. 3)
1. 6   2. 12   3. 18   4. 24   5. 30
6. 36   7. 42   8. 48   9. 54   10. 60

Multiples 2 (p. 3)
1. 8   2. 16   3. 24   4. 32   5. 40
6. 48   7. 56   8. 64   9. 72   10. 80

Multiples 3 (p. 3)
1. 11   2. 22   3. 33   4. 44   5. 55
6. 66   7. 77   8. 88   9. 99   10. 110

Multiples 4 (p. 4)
1. 4, 6, 8, 10, 12   2. 6, 9, 12, 15, 18
3. 8, 12, 16, 20, 24   4. 10, 15, 20, 25, 30
5. 14, 21, 28, 35, 42   6. 18, 27, 36, 45, 54

Multiples 5 (p. 4)
1. 20, 30, 40, 50, 60   2. 28, 42, 56, 70, 84
3. 40, 60, 80, 100, 120   4. 36, 54, 72, 90, 108
5. 24, 36, 48, 60, 72
6. 50, 75, 100, 125, 150

Multiples 6 (p. 4)
1. Yes   2. No   3. Yes   4. No   5. No
6. Yes

Multiples 7 (p. 4)
1. 0   2. 8   3. 0   4. 7   5. 0
6. 12   7. 0   8. 2   9. 0   10. 5

Multiplying by a Single Digit 1 (p. 5)
1. 669   2. 228   3. 969   4. 1,676

Multiplying by a Single Digit 2 (p. 5)
1. 3,380   2. 1,824   3. 3,708   4. 1,794

Multiplying by a Single Digit 3 (p. 5)
1. 6,939   2. 3,605   3. 747   4 2,536

Multiplying by a Single Digit 4 (p. 5)
1. 8,991   2. 707   3. 4,220   4. 3,184

Multiplying by a Single Digit 5 (p. 6)
1. 4,248   2. 3,608   3. 2,456   4. 2,412

Multiplying by 10 1 (p. 6)
1. 750   2. 1,450   3. 9,000   4. 22,400

Multiplying by 10 2 (p. 6)
1. 3,130   2. 5,550   3. 10,000 4. 1,020

Multiplying by 10 3 (p. 7)
1. 250   2. 1,500   3. 8,000   4. 22,500

Multiplying by 10 4 (p. 7)
1. 130,000   2. 8,250   3. 500   4. 1,750

Multiplying by 10 5 (p. 7)
1. 320   2. 780   3. 6,890   4. 3,250

Multiplying by Two Digits 1 (p. 8)
1. 5,313   2. 4,444   3. 5,124   4. 8,180

Multiplying by Two Digits 2 (p. 8)
1. 51,870   2. 27,166
3. 16,800   4. 388,875

Multiplying by Two Digits 3 (p. 8)
1. 115,500   2. 7,392
3. 4,848   4. 419,976

Multiplying by Two Digits 4 (p. 8)
1. 51,975   2. 35,505
3. 28,350   4. 61,440

Multiplying by Two Digits 5 (p. 9)
1. 25,245   2. 2,239,872
3. 42,294   4. 1,845

Multiplying by Three Digits 1 (p. 9)
1. 28,408   2. 15,561   3. 224,775

Multiplying by Three Digits 2 (p. 9)
1. 115,620   2. 702,119   3. 1,606,500

Multiplying by Three Digits 3 (p. 10)
1. 309,465   2. 1,308,000
3. 24,150,000

Multiplying by Three Digits 4 (p. 10)
1. 1,111,505   2. 882,000
3. 6,890,000

Multiplying by Three Digits 5 (p. 10)
1. 346,545   2. 106,215   3. 97,047

Multiplying Integers 1 (p. 11)
1. -72   2. 36   3. 40
4. -21   5. -240   6. -12

Multiplying Integers 2 (p. 11)
1. -91   2. 375   3. -96
4. 12   5. 72   6. -126

Multiplying Integers 3 (p. 11)
1. -2,888   2. -2,720   3. 16,116   4. 3,256

Multiplying Integers 4 (p. 11)
1. -133,750   2. 540 3. -9,050   4. 4,448

Multiplying by 100, 1,000, or More 1 (p. 12)
1. 7,500   2. 451,000
3. 15,420,000

Multiplying by 100, 1,000, or More 2 (p. 12)
1. 3,400   2. 25,500   3. 51,500
4. 885,000   5. 650,000   6. 3,750,000
7. 10,000,000

Multiplying by 100, 1,000, or More 3 (p. 12)
1. 6,500   2. 3,500   3. 78,500
4. 52,500

Multiplying by 100, 1,000, or More 4 (p. 12)
1. 955,000   2. 1,500,000   3. 350,000
4. 250,000

Multiplying by 100, 1,000, or More 5 (p. 13)
1. 6,500,000   2. 20,000,000
3. 75,000   4. 20,000,000

Multiplying With Decimals 1 (p. 13)
1. 396   2. 6,890.7
3. 6,597.50   4. 8,016

Multiplying With Decimals 2 (p. 13)
1. 6,100   2. 13,359.6
3. 886.288   4. 630

Multiplying With Decimals 3 (p. 13)
1. 8,797.50   2. 23,157.50
3. 10,904   4. 10,038.65

Multiplying With Decimals 4 (p. 14)
1. 1,578.444   2. 437.5
3. 1.62   4. 859.375

Multiplying With Decimals 5 (p. 14)
1. 160,171   2. 0.08415
3. 707   4. 1.989

Multiplying a Fraction by a Fraction 1 (p. 14)
1. $\frac{35}{48}$ 2. $\frac{5}{72}$ 3. $\frac{2}{5}$ 4. $\frac{2}{5}$
5. $\frac{9}{32}$ 6. $\frac{7}{25}$

Multiplying a Fraction by a Fraction 2 (p. 15)
1. $\frac{9}{50}$ 2. $\frac{2}{3}$ 3. $\frac{21}{40}$ 4. $\frac{1}{4}$

Multiplying a Fraction by a Fraction 3 (p. 15)
1. $\frac{7}{10}$ 2. $\frac{21}{50}$ 3. $\frac{15}{32}$ 4. $\frac{3}{16}$

Multiplying a Fraction by a Fraction 4 (p. 15)
1. $\frac{8}{25}$ 2. $\frac{8}{15}$ 3. $\frac{1}{6}$ 4. $\frac{1}{6}$

Multiplying a Fraction by a Fraction 5 (p. 15)
1. $\frac{21}{80}$ 2. $\frac{9}{16}$ 3. $\frac{1}{2}$ 4. $\frac{2}{9}$

Multiplying Fractions & Whole Numbers 1 (p. 16)
1. 1   2. $11\frac{2}{5}$ 3. $11\frac{1}{2}$ 4. $9\frac{1}{6}$

Multiplying Fractions & Whole Numbers 2 (p. 16)
1. $\frac{1}{2}$ 2. $7\frac{3}{4}$ 3. $10\frac{2}{3}$ 4. $1\frac{1}{2}$

Multiplying Fractions & Whole Numbers 3 (p. 16)
1. $5\frac{2}{3}$ 2. 5   3. $4\frac{1}{2}$ 4. $12\frac{1}{4}$

Multiplying Fractions & Whole Numbers 4 (p. 17)
1. $10\frac{1}{2}$ 2. $6\frac{3}{10}$ 3. $\frac{1}{2}$ 4. 28

Multiplying Fractions & Whole Numbers 5 (p. 17)
1. 3   2. $2\frac{4}{5}$ 3. 3   4. $\frac{5}{9}$

Multiplying Mixed Numbers 1 (p. 17)
1. $12\frac{1}{2}$ 2. 20   3. 15   4. $12\frac{3}{8}$

Multiplying Mixed Numbers 2 (p. 18)
1. $3\frac{8}{9}$ 2. $12\frac{1}{4}$ 3. $3\frac{3}{5}$ 4. $11\frac{1}{4}$

Multiplying Mixed Numbers 3 (p. 18)

1. 6   2. $12\frac{1}{2}$ 3. $7\frac{7}{8}$ 4. $16\frac{2}{3}$

Multiplying Mixed Numbers 4 (p. 18)

1. $3\frac{11}{18}$ 2. 4   3. 9   4. $4\frac{1}{8}$

Multiplying Mixed Numbers 5 (p. 18)

1. $8\frac{2}{5}$ 2. 13   3. $16\frac{7}{8}$ 4. $61\frac{1}{5}$

Multiplying Fractions & Mixed Numbers: A Shortcut 1 (p. 19)

1. $\frac{3}{10}$ 2. $1\frac{1}{10}$ 3. $\frac{2}{9}$ 4. $1\frac{1}{2}$

5. 3   6. $\frac{3}{16}$

Multiplying Fractions & Mixed Numbers: A Shortcut 2 (p. 19)

1. $\frac{7}{15}$ 2. $2\frac{1}{2}$ 3. $\frac{4}{5}$ 4. $\frac{5}{18}$

Multiplying Fractions & Mixed Numbers: A Shortcut 3 (p. 19)

1. $\frac{3}{4}$ 2. $\frac{7}{15}$ 3. $\frac{14}{15}$ 4. 1

Multiplication Review 1 (p. 20)

1. 105   2. 108   3. 246
4. 560   5. 399   6. 392

Multiplication Review 2 (p. 20)

1.   2.

Multiplication Review 3 (p. 20)

1. <   2. <   3. >   4. <   5. =   6. >
7. <   8. =

Multiplication Review 4 (p. 21)

1. 24   2. 56   3. 54   4. 35   5. 64   6. 66
7. 48   8. 200

Multiplication Review 5 (p. 21)

1. 574   2. 2,944   3. 1,944   4. 1,936

Multiplication Review 6 (p. 21)

1. $\frac{2}{9}$ 2. $\frac{3}{28}$ 3. $\frac{5}{36}$

4. $\frac{1}{48}$ 5. $\frac{1}{72}$ 6. $\frac{15}{56}$

Multiplication Review 7 (p. 21)

1. 18.13   2. 33.06   3. 34.31
4. 11.92   5. 25,437.645   6. 258,956.88

Dividing Made Easier: Factors 1 (p. 22)

1. 1, 2, 3, 4, 6, 12   2. 1, 2, 4, 8, 16, 32

Dividing Made Easier: Factors 2 (p. 22)

1. 1, 3, 5, 9, 15, 45   2. prime   3. prime
4. 1, 2, 4, 5, 10, 20, 25, 50, 100

Dividing Made Easier: Factors 3 (p. 22)

1. 1, 2, 3, 4, 5, 6, 8, 10, 12, 15, 20, 24, 30, 40, 60, 120
2. 1, 3, 5, 15   3. 1, 2, 31, 62
4. 1, 3, 19, 57

Dividing Made Easier: Factors 4 (p. 23)

1–5.   Answers will vary. Teacher check that the two numbers multiplied result in the original number.

Dividing Made Easier: Factors 5 (p. 23)

1–5.   Answers will vary. Teacher check that the two numbers multiplied result in the original number.

Division Models 1 (p. 23)

6 sets of 6

Division Models 2 (p. 23)

5 sets of 3

Division Models 3 (p. 24)

3 sets of 10 with 5 items left over

Division Models 4 (p. 24)

5 sets of 12 with 4 items left over

Dividing by Single Digits 1 (p. 24)

1. 101   2. 130

Dividing by Single Digits 2 (p. 24)

1. 115 r5   2. 88

Dividing by Single Digits 3 (p. 25)

1. 336 R1   2. 66 R5

Dividing by Single Digits 4 (p. 25)

1. 325   2. 117

Dividing by Single Digits 5 (p. 25)

1. 262   2. 225   3. 81

Dividing by Single Digits 6 (p. 25)

1. 206 R1   2. 140 R1   3. 127 R1

Remainders 1 (p. 26)

1. $55\frac{4}{9}$ 2. $1,562\frac{1}{5}$

Remainders 2 (p. 26)

1. $78\frac{1}{8}$ 2. $33\frac{1}{4}$ 3. $627\frac{1}{2}$ 4. $92\frac{3}{6}$

Remainders 3 (p. 26)

1. 126 2. $141\frac{2}{5}$ 3. $84\frac{3}{8}$ 4. $37\frac{2}{4}$

Remainders 4 (p. 26)

1. $166\frac{6}{9}$ 2. 175 3. $47\frac{4}{8}$ 4. $1,350$

Remainders 5 (p. 27)

1. $55\frac{5}{9}$ 2. $1,978\frac{3}{4}$ 3. $92\frac{6}{7}$ 4. $433\frac{1}{3}$

Dividing by Two Digits 1 (p. 27)

1. $47\frac{4}{13}$ 2. $9\frac{28}{40}$ 3. $8\frac{42}{75}$

Dividing by Two Digits 2 (p. 27)

1. $32\frac{7}{31}$ 2. $68\frac{35}{90}$ 3. $216\frac{10}{15}$

Dividing by Two Digits 3 (p. 28)

1. $950\frac{24}{28}$ 2. $906\frac{48}{67}$ 3. $188\frac{68}{89}$

Dividing by Two Digits 4 (p. 28)

1. $1,000$ 2. 250 3. $2,666\frac{32}{48}$

Dividing by Two Digits 5 (p. 28)

1. $27\frac{3}{25}$ 2. $888\frac{10}{30}$ 3. $64\frac{70}{95}$

Dividing by 10 1 (p. 29)
1. 85 2. 39 3. 450 4. 105
5. $4,300$

Dividing by 10 2 (p. 29)
1. $1,230$ 2. 92 3. 83 4. 720
5. $6,550$

Dividing by 10 3 (p. 29)
1. 74 2. 61 3. 152 4. 310
5. $2,800$

Dividing by 10 4 (p. 29)
1. 50 2. 48 3. 643 4. $2,971$
5. $52,590$

Dividing by 100 or 1,000 1 (p. 30)
1. 30 2. 50 3. 12 4. 88
5. 15

Dividing by 100 or 1,000 2 (p. 30)
1. 255 2. 25 3. 99 4. 25 5. 725

Dividing by 100 or 1,000 3 (p. 30)
1. 40 2. 56 3. 300 4. 45 5. 178

Dividing by 100 or 1,000 4 (p. 30)
1. 91 2. 680 3. 57 4. 79 5. 432

Dividing by Three Digits 1 (p. 31)
1. $18\frac{105}{125}$ 2. $3\frac{267}{344}$ 3. $11\frac{22}{188}$

Dividing by Three Digits 2 (p. 31)
1. $2\frac{290}{900}$ 2. $36\frac{250}{375}$ 3. 12

Dividing by Three Digits 3 (p. 31)
1. $1\frac{201}{899}$ 2. $29\frac{233}{641}$ 3. $291\frac{645}{705}$

Dividing by Three Digits 4 (p. 32)
1. $36\frac{165}{202}$ 2. $27\frac{344}{512}$ 3. $1,581\frac{488}{615}$

Dividing by Three Digits 5 (p. 32)
1. $192\frac{273}{333}$ 2. $72\frac{111}{176}$ 3. $782\frac{221}{224}$

Dividing Integers 1 (p. 32)
1. -42 2. $-383\frac{14}{234}$ 3. $803\frac{5}{8}$

Dividing Integers 2 (p. 33)
1. -629 2. $-4,288\frac{3}{17}$ 3. $1,985\frac{160}{414}$

Dividing Integers 3 (p. 33)
1. $-1,639\frac{40}{44}$ 2. $6,931\frac{8}{9}$ 3. $-494\frac{37}{65}$

Dividing Integers 4 (p. 33)
1. $3,595\frac{55}{112}$ 2. $-2\frac{79}{82}$ 3. $-301\frac{41}{91}$

Dividing Integers 5 (p. 34)
1. -4 2. 2 3. -9 4. 2 5. 4 6. -6

Dividing Integers 6 (p. 34)
1. 7 2. -3 3. 7 4. -4 5. -3 6. 3

Converting Fractions to Decimals 1 (p. 34)
1. 0.8333 2. 0.5667 3. 0.04
4. 0.45 5. 0.96 6. 0.9085

Converting Fractions to Decimals 2 (p. 35)
1. 0.875 2. 0.0714 3. 0.6667
4. 0.9167 5. 0.2692

Converting Fractions to Decimals 3 (p. 35)
1. 3.375 2. 10.8421 3. 24.3119
4. 59.1111 5. 164.8452

Converting Fractions to Decimals 4 (p. 35)
1. 185.425 2. 44.18 3. 16.875
4. 194.85 5. 5.997

Converting Fractions to Decimals 5 (p. 35)
1. 7.8 2. 10.25 3. 25.2273
4. 190.5714 5. 16.95

Dividing With Decimals 1 (p. 36)
1. 72 2. 41 3. 108

Dividing With Decimals 2 (p. 36)
1. 62 2. 88

Dividing With Decimals 3 (p. 36)
1. 75 2. 18

Dividing With Decimals 4 (p. 37)
1. 40 2. 136

Dividing With Decimals 5 (p. 37)
1. 183 2. 71

Dividing With Decimals 6 (p. 37)
1. 100.1 2. 128.6

Dividing With Decimals 7 (p. 37)
1. 77 2. 199

Dividing With Fractions: Reciprocals 1 (p. 38)
1. $\frac{7}{3}$ 2. $\frac{4}{5}$ 3. $\frac{8}{7}$ 4. $\frac{1}{7}$

Dividing With Fractions: Reciprocals 2 (p. 38)
1. $\frac{4}{39}$ 2. $\frac{1}{21}$ 3. $\frac{6}{5}$ 4. $\frac{2}{29}$
5. $\frac{5}{4}$ 6. $\frac{5}{48}$

Dividing With Fractions: Reciprocals 3 (p. 38)
1. $\frac{3}{2}$ 2. $\frac{1}{73}$ 3. $\frac{1}{5}$ 4. $\frac{6}{31}$
5. $\frac{12}{1}$ 6. $\frac{3}{31}$

Dividing by Fractions 1 (p. 39)
1. $2\frac{2}{3}$ 2. $\frac{5}{8}$ 3. $1\frac{2}{7}$ 4. $\frac{24}{35}$

Dividing by Fractions 2 (p. 39)
1. $1\frac{4}{5}$ 2. $\frac{18}{25}$ 3. $1\frac{7}{8}$ 4. 4

Dividing by Fractions 3 (p. 39)
1. $\frac{8}{9}$ 2. $\frac{5}{12}$ 3. $\frac{15}{32}$ 4. $\frac{1}{3}$

Dividing by Fractions 4 (p. 40)
1. 1 2. $\frac{1}{4}$ 3. $\frac{3}{8}$ 4. $\frac{3}{20}$

Dividing by Fractions 5 (p. 40)
1. $\frac{3}{4}$ 2. $1\frac{1}{4}$ 3. $12\frac{1}{4}$ 4. $1\frac{1}{4}$

Dividing Whole Numbers & Mixed Numbers 1 (p. 40)
1. 5 2. 10 3. $\frac{5}{16}$ 4. $\frac{9}{10}$

Dividing Whole Numbers & Mixed Numbers 2 (p. 41)
1. $\frac{3}{8}$ 2. $3\frac{1}{8}$ 3. 2 4. $4\frac{1}{2}$

Dividing Whole Numbers & Mixed Numbers 3 (p. 41)
1. 3 2. $\frac{9}{35}$ 3. $1\frac{2}{7}$ 4. $\frac{5}{6}$

Dividing Whole Numbers & Mixed Numbers 4 (p. 41)
1. 8 2. 6 3. $\frac{25}{36}$ 4. 24

Dividing Whole Numbers & Mixed Numbers 5 (p. 41)
1. $2\frac{2}{3}$ 2. 3 3. $17\frac{1}{2}$ 4. $\frac{20}{27}$

Division Review 1 (p. 42)

1. 3	2. 7	3. 7	4. 7
7	6	6	8
15	9	8	3
18	12	4	4
6	4	11	9

Division Review 2 (p. 42)
1. 88; 88 x 6 = 528 2. 65; 65 x 7 = 455
3. 114; 114 x 12 = 1,368

Division Review 3 (p. 42)
1. 7 2. 7 3. 6

Division Review 4 (p. 43)
1. 9 2. 9 3. 8 4. 7 5. 4 6. 6

Division Review 5 (p. 43)
1. 11 R6 2. 12 R3 3. 3 R3
4. 25 R1 5. 8 R3 6. 10 R4

Division Review 6 (p. 43)

1. $\frac{1}{3}$ 2. $1\frac{1}{2}$ 3. 2   4. $\frac{1}{56}$ 5. $\frac{40}{63}$

Division Review 7 (p. 43)

1. 3.6   2. 3.6   3. 8.59   4. 17.52
5. 509.34   6. 11,056.86

Multiplication Word Problems 1 (p. 44)

1. $51   2. 108   3. 252

Multiplication Word Problems 2 (p. 44)

1. 12   2. 21   3. 112

Multiplication Word Problems 3 (p. 44)

1. 224   2. 869   3. 315   4. 112

Multiplication Word Problems 4 (p. 45)

1. 1,125   2. 1,800

Multiplication Word Problems 5 (p. 45)

1. $1.15   2. $15.96   3. $137.84

Multiplication Word Problems 6 (p. 45)

1. $57   2. $292   3. $162   4. $830

Multiplication Word Problems 7 (p. 46)

1. 1,116   2. $2,790   3. $1,674
4. $4,464

Multiplication Word Problems 8 (p. 46)

1. $1.72   2. $2.93   3. $5.20

Multiplication Word Problems 9 (p. 46)

1. 25.9 miles   2. 285 pies

Multiplication Word Problems 10 (p. 47)

1. 75,000   2. 72,000

Multiplication Word Problems 11 (p. 47)

1. $\frac{4}{9}$ cup   2. $3\frac{1}{3}$ bushels

Multiplication Word Problems 12 (p. 47)

1. $4\frac{1}{5}$ miles   2. 2 trays

Multiplication Word Problems 13 (p. 47)

1. 52 ounces   2. $8.44

Division Word Problems 1 (p. 48)

1. 12   2. 48   3. 69   4. 476

Division Word Problems 2 (p. 48)

1. 12   2. 51   3. 21

Division Word Problems 3 (p. 48)

Answers can be in any order. Possible answers:

1 – 80   2 – 40   4 – 20   5 – 16
8 – 10   10 – 8   16 – 5   20 – 4
40 – 2   80 – 1

Division Word Problems 4 (p. 49)

1. 52   2. 107.5

Division Word Problems 5 (p. 49)

70

Division Word Problems 6 (p. 49)

1. 54.9   2. 30

Division Word Problems 7 (p. 49)

1. $4,500   2. $140

Division Word Problems 8 (p. 50)

1. 1,500   2. 140

Division Word Problems 9 (p. 50)

1. 225   2. 308 yards

Division Word Problems 10 (p. 50)

1. $383\frac{155}{215}$ or 383.72
There cannot be a partial package, so there were approximately 384 packages per route.
2. 34

Division Word Problems 11 (p. 51)

1. 3   2. 2

Division Word Problems 12 (p. 51)

1. 19   2. 45

Division Word Problems 13 (p. 51)

1. 24   2. 8

Division Word Problems 14 (p. 51)

1. 3   2. $6\frac{1}{2}$

Mixed-Operation Word Problems 1 (p. 52)

1. 10 hours   2. $54

Mixed-Operation Word Problems 2 (p. 52)

1. two for $1.49   2. one for $1.13

Mixed-Operation Word Problems 3 (p. 52)

1. $113.26   2. $12.50

Mixed-Operation Word Problems 4 (p. 52)

1. $4.15   2. $4.60

Mixed-Operation Word Problems 5 (p. 53)
1. 42
2. 42 x 5 = 210
3. 52 cards with 2 left over
4. 52 x 4 = 208 + 2 = 210

Mixed-Operation Word Problems 6 (p. 53)

1. 10   2. $2\frac{1}{2}$

3. $3\frac{3}{4}$ 4. 5

Mixed-Operation Word Problems 7 (p. 54)
Jeremy should deliver approximately 26
packages a day.

Mixed-Operation Word Problems 8 (p. 54)
138 ÷ 67 = 2.059; 2 x 67 = 134;
138 - 134 = 4 on the last page;
They will put two pictures on each page and
four pictures on the last page.

Mixed-Operation Word Problems 9 (p. 54)
878 ÷ 3 = 292.67;
She can make 292 full bags of cookies.
292 x $0.75 = $219;
She can make $219.

Bibliography

Exercises may have appeared in one of the following previously published books:

Armstrong, Linda. (2008) *Daily Skill Builders: Word Problems.* Mark Twain Media, Inc., Publishers.

Barden, Cindy. (2005) *Jumpstarters for Math.* Mark Twain Media, Inc., Publishers.

Cameron, Schyrlet and Carolyn Craig. (2014) *All About Decimals: Math for CCSS Grades 5–8.* Mark Twain Media, Inc., Publishers.

Cameron, Schyrlet and Carolyn Craig. (2013) *Multiplying and Dividing Fractions: Grades 5–8.* Mark Twain Media, Inc., Publishers.

Owen, M.J. (2003) *Math Engagement: Grade 5.* Mark Twain Media, Inc., Publishers.

Torrance, Hal. (2011) *Math Tutor: Multiplication & Division.* Mark Twain Media, Inc., Publishers.